Where the Wild Roses Grow

A Collection of Poetry and Prose for the Heart of a Woman

VOLUME II

Gaia Rose

ISBN: 978-1-8380554-6-2

Front cover image by
Olga Korneeva/shutterstock.com

Frontispiece wild rose image by
AVA Bitter/shutterstock.com

Poem pages rose image by
lisima/shutterstock.com

I dedicate 'Volume II' of my poetry and prose collection to the millions of beautifully courageous wild women, mothers, and daughters who have marched by my side in protest against unjust laws, wrongful oppression, and stripping of our birth given rights.

I will forever hold you in my heart as we stand together unified around the world in our continued fight for truth, liberation, and freedom.

Preface

If you know me, and know my heart, then you'll also know who I am and who I am not – a woman of truth, a woman who has an opinion, a woman of authenticity and integrity, a woman of no bullshit, a woman with strong morals, values, and beliefs, a woman who has survived more challenges than most, a woman of the wild earth, and a woman who understands the sacredness of life and how it is meant to be lived with daring risk and unwavering faith. So, I shall ask for no forgiveness to whom my words may trigger, I shall make no apologies to where my weaved words flow, and I shall no longer hide away the courage and conviction within my own integrity to forever express the freedom within *my* heart of truth - as anything less than this would not be *me*.

The poetry and prose within this second volume of mine is no doubt more powerfully written, more *wild*, and offers much more of a feminine *roar* than volume I. Many of these poems (if not all) were written between 2020-2022, when, like many, my *'inner seasons'* became incredibly raw (and continue to be at times) from the trauma and triumph that my wild free-spirited soul was bravely breaking through at such a dark time in history. Nearly all poems have already been shared publicly before this book was even published - *alongside my voice* – at times getting me judged, shamed, and silenced, especially in 2020 -2021, which sadly is always going to be a human truth that crashes down upon those of us who are courageous enough to speak up, go against societies voice, and dare to be the difference in a world forever trying to take us from our individuality. *But,* sharing my heart in this most authentic raw way (more than I ever have before) has also connected me with my *true* tribe, the women (and men) that share my own core values, whilst inspiring many others to also speak their truth, stand up for what they individually know in their heart to be right, and *never* feel coerced, bullied, or compromised in their own integrity.

The truth is, people that live in fear, in ignorance, and in blind conformity will always be scared of what they don't understand, they will always shame what they themselves haven't had the courage to question, and they will never truly break free from the cage they are in until they are truly ready to *see* - with their hearts as well as their eyes.

I've come to find that there is something beautiful about writing our truth in poetic form that doesn't quite seem to 'trigger' as deeply as if it were simply just written down. I'm not sure why...maybe it's because poetry is very much like a song, a story, a tale of truth, that even when others disagree they can't help but still be captured by the *weaved beauty* within its flow. Who knows? Either way, this is just one of the many reasons I am passionate about expressing my written word through poetry, as it allows my heart to spill out in the form of '*spoken song*' – sharing the soul of my own spirit, whilst returning others to the soul within theirs.

I hope the following poems and '*poetic short stories*' of mine guide and align you back to your heart, inspire you to always protect the beauty within your *own* sovereignty, and remind you that you are *never* alone in your courageous and commendable fight for truth, for justice, for freedom.

Gaia Rose

International Woman's Day -
March 8th, 2022

"Her wild feminine heart would rather die fighting for a life of freedom, than live conforming to a caged oppression"

Rebirthing Her Tribe...

...Her inner and outer circle, the women and men she held close were no longer what it was before. The energy of the awakened hearts, fierce warriors, and *true* authentic souls of the earth were the only ones she now welcomed into her own awakened door. The teachers, speakers, authors, healers, friendships and family she once admired, looked up to, and believed were *true* in spirit were no longer what she thought. Ashamed to have ever given time to such fakers, takers of external validation and praise, even if it meant becoming who they were *not*, all now preaching the word of the masses, the way of the needy, and the false science propaganda paid for by the greedy, ignorantly turning their back on mother natures way and all the ancient wisdom of what it means to be an individual, human, sovereign soul.

The divide was clear, it was already here, showing up all those who held fear behind their eyes, and those who held freedom. Those who liked to please the outside, and those who stood for integrity - strong in their authentic King and *Queen*dom. Those who understood the precious meaning of life, and those who would never understand, no matter how much truth she placed within their hand, their closed conforming hearts would remain blind to it all.

So with sadness behind her eyes and surrender within each of her sighs, she *re*-birthed her organic tribe of sisters, mothers, sons and brothers, finding safety and comfort in only the rebel hearts, the fearless voice, the truth speakers who stood for individual choice, and those courageous enough to remember how to be an original human being, as these were the only ones that made her feel *seen*, accepted, and protected...
from the now,
broken,
world.

Arrow And Bow

Ignorant in their sleep, believing only which they are told, too tired to seek the truth themselves in their blind conforming world.
Living to please the crowd, to be part of illusion and lies, so they continue to shame and maim all those who speak with awakened eyes.
Waiting to be told, waiting to be led, whilst *her* wild heart stands only for freedom, fighting for life instead.

So she learns to now ignore, all those who don't want to hear, continuing to speak her truth, without shame, doubt, or fear.
Wisely planting the seed, in her own authentic way, no longer forcing those who aren't ready to awaken upon this day.
Just trusting in *her* truth, and all *her* heart reveals, listening to *her* inner voice and the way her own soul feels.
Because ignorant *she* is not, as she holds up her arrow and bow -

"For a life without choice, without freedom of voice, is truly NO life at all"

She Shall Not Bow Down...

...Whether in body or spirit, to anyone upon the Earth.
She shall not fall to her knees to prove where *she* stands.
She shall not be subservient to those with hearts full of fear, control, and insecurities.
She shall not follow the crowds unsteady forceful flow, but rather her own flow of feminine freedom.
She shall not be told who *she* is, simply because her life's dance is different than the rest.
She shall not quieten her voice, her opinions, or her individual mind simply because someone somewhere will be offended.
She shall not deny her own inner hearts peace so that others can feel more comfortable with theirs.

No...

She shall not bow down....

She shall never betray or stray from her own hearts' truth, her own inner alignment, and her own beautiful path. A path that forever only answers to the Mother, the moon, the stars, the wind, the water, the fire and the Earth -

A great wild source of true freedom from which 'she' was beautifully birthed.

In Her Wild

They say her truth is wrong,
They believe her choices are weak,
Even though they won't question the hypocrisy and lies which they themselves haven't took time to seek.

They say her words are cruel,
They choose to *not* understand,
They'd rather live in 'comfortable fear' than to challenge the evil of man.

They say her heart is cold,
When *she* chooses *not* to comply,
Walking around unmasked, unjabbed, from coercion injustice and lies.

As *they* would rather be wrongly oppressed,
With their ignorance, compliance, and fear,
Never daring to fight for what's morally right,
Never doubting the 'leaders' they hear.

But *she* shall forever carry on 'in her *wild*',
Being the good against humanities sin,
For she would rather be free from a fucked society –

Uncaged from the cage *they* are in.

Embracing *Her* Craziness…

…Was the most sanest thing she had ever done.

Weather The Tide

She sees what others won't,
She acts how others don't,
She speaks and fights for all that's right even when it leaves her broke.
She knows the depth of suffering,
She's felt the deepest despair,
But continues to stand for liberty and life when others stand in oppression and fear.

She knows the unseen truth,
She shares it where she can,
Forever called to break down the wall where others won't lend a hand.
Because *she* is a woman of heart,
Of integrity, justice and pride,
Courageously free in a caged society -

Unafraid to weather the tide.

She Dares To Live...

...Where others sit back in silence, *she* dares to be heard,
Where others are too afraid to stand up for what's right, *she* dares to fight,
And where others are blinded by the lies, *she* dares to speak the truth,
As her wild, courageous, untamed heart forever reminds her through deep inner whispers of sweet songs -

"Only those who dare to be brave enough to truly live, shall live FREE!"

Uncomfortable Wildness

They believed she was selfish.
Selfish for not conforming to an unfree world.
Selfish for not thinking more of others than she did of herself.
Selfish for being a rebel, an outcast, and a woman with no boundaries that created fear in their heart of rules.

"*How dare she!*" They would mutter underneath their masks aplenty, desperately believing *they* are the ones 'saving humanity', ignorantly turning their wilful blindness towards her 'uncomfortable wildness', hoping to block out the truth which *they* are too fearful to see.

For it was the beautiful bravery within *her* 'selfishness' that showed up *their* lack of courage –

to live, to fight back, to be *free!*

Unbecoming

They no longer liked her...
Not like before.
They no longer saw her how they used to.
The kindness in her expression seemed edgy.
The truth in how she spoke seemed to more deeply provoke.
And her presence seemed more powerful, but not in a way they could understand.

Maybe she was just UNbecoming - stripping herself bare from years of the societal conditioning *they* had.
Maybe she was just stepping into her fullest self, a self that was not good, nor bad.

Or maybe she had finally found the brave parts of who she always was, hiding behind the smile, underneath the sad. All lingering within the curves of her body, the sway of her hips, the wild authentic voice flowing out from her full womanly lips, awaiting for her to birth every beautiful bit.

Still...

They no longer liked her…
But it was ok.
She no longer liked them either.

A Woman Of Difference

Being a woman of difference meant she needed to question everything.
She wouldn't just accept what she was told.
And why should she?
Her curious wild heart was born to live individually.
For it were her questions that became the soil which seeded the roots of who she was becoming...
...Untamed. Liberated. Free.

Being a woman of difference wasn't just courageous -

It was fucking beautiful!

Weaved Beneath Her Skin

The rush of the risk was worth more than anything ever set in stone,
To courageously *live* in a world that tries to diminish her creative soul,
To rebel against the ignorance, the fear, and the blind society she has come to know,
To dance out the wildness of her inner fire, with sovereignty, faith, and flow.
For this was *her* freedom...
A freedom that reminded her she is not caged by woman nor man,
A freedom that returned her to peace, to joy, to the rights that show *she* can,
A freedom that could never truly be taken, stripped down, or broken-in,
For *her* freedom was already written and weaved –

Weaved beneath her skin.

Sovereign And Free Was She...

...Breathing in the green fields that birthed
the daisies and wild flowers,
Far away from all she has ever known.
Her *true* home.

No faces masked or man made rules to adhere to,
Just her own naked smile - *rebel style* - gazing at the
sunlit sky as it rises above the swaying trees, whilst
dew drops say goodbye to the morning breeze.
Birthing a brand new day.

"Can this be my forever?"
Her heart whispers into the bluebirds wing as it
dances by the heathers,
Bringing a song of peace for her soul to sing,
Allowing this perfect stillness to be her everything.
Just for a moment...
...She sinks further into the Earths ocean of nature,
forgetting the world and the sadness of what was
once before,
As the Mother gifts her with healing waves of
everlasting freedom,
A freedom that would carry her home -

Gently back home to shore.

Only A Woman

She holds her head high, with tears in her eyes, and
strength carved upon her fierce tongue,
Keeps her voice loud and proud, standing true
amongst the crowd, letting them know her rise has
begun.

A woman who's journeyed far, survived every scar, yet
the sadness weighs hard on her soul,
Tired in each breath, at times longing for
death, though her fight will not allow her to fall.

For she is only a woman, who bleeds, ebbs, and
flows, born with courage weaved under her skin.
So cry - *for all the unjust,*
Rest - *if you must,*
But darling, don't you *dare* let those fuckers win!

She Doesn't Have To Justify Her "NO!"

...NO to health choices and decisions,
NO to her reasons or rhyme,
NO to anyone or anything that does not add value to her time.

NO to the lies and the fears,
NO to the majority's 'way',
NO to opinions that don't meet with her own,
courageous in all she may say.

NO to the masks and 'injections',
NO to *all* that's bad for *her* health,
NO to the coercion and shaming her flow, as she has the *right* to decide for herself.

NO to the 'experts' and doctors,
NO to the false leaders of man,
NO to all those who only follow *one* voice, being the difference wherever *she* can.

NO to the bullshit and hypocrisy,
NO to 'off' vibes and fake news,
NO to any destruction that breaks down her soul,

for she shall *never* partake in abuse.

Because NO is a sentence said fully,
And NO explanation should be needed to hear,
For her life and her choice is *hers* only,
Choosing *freedom,* where others choose *fear.*

They Can Never Break Her Smile...

...An inner smile *gifted* to her from birth.
Just as her right to peace was gifted – *gifted to her from within* - so is her right to *all* beauty that lays beneath her skin.
From the untouched part of her soul that can never truly be broken,
From the unseen essence forever flowing out from many weaved words unspoken,
From the inner sacred space of truth that *knows* all, *feels* all, and *reveals* all, when she's lost her way...

This was always her most precious creation, her most treasured strength, her most fierce liberation, and it was from this birth given expression-of-self, residing inside of her own spiritual unique-ness, that her beauty could continue to flow however *she* chose, even through the darkness of others, for no man nor woman could ever truly claim this sacred part of her human existence.

So let them make their rules,
Let them silence her voice,
Let them place their oppression and lies upon her freedom of choice...

Haven't they realised yet?
Her heart still individually *feels,* even though they don't want it to,
Her wild soul still rises and *heals,* after all the pain they've put her through,
And her rebellious expression, still unapologetically real - *authentic, courageous, and true.*

So you see, they can never *truly* break her smile...

For it was *never* theirs to take.

Beautifully Unmasked...

...Wrapped up in her bubble of non-conformity, naked expressions, and open gestures, as she wildly weaves authentically amongst the faceless crowd, the hidden smiles, and the fearful hearts oppressed behind their proud masks of many colours, all standing happily in their ignorance and denial, not wanting to upset the 'team', seem 'unfashionable', or sway from societies voice, as they endlessly and emptily repeat to themselves *"we must follow the rules"*. Like a flowing stream of innocent children who can't find their own way home unless their 'master' allows. Never daring to *question*, never stopping to *see*, never pondering upon their mass *conformity*, or even asking themselves *"when is enough, enough, for me?"*

So she courageously continues to pull down the masks – *metaphorically and otherwise* - defending her own inner and outer curiosity, being the mirror, the light, the trigger, so that others may *know*, so that others may *choose*, so that others may *fight*, so that others may *feel* with their own intuitive heart *all* that is right, whilst *she* proudly portrays a rebellious nature with her expressionate mouth unapologetically in sight, greeting all who cross her path, desperately hoping to pour a moment of remembrance back into their soulless caged eyes of what it *means* to be human, what it *means* to be free, what it *means* to be unique, what it *means* to be unshackled from the hypocrisy, unjust laws, and mountains of lies that their ego *longs* to keep, as *she* breaks through each boundary with the deepest peace growing inside - a wolf amongst the sheep…

Beautifully *unmasked.*

"Where Have All The Humans Gone?" ...

...She wonders, as she reminisces upon a time where the soul was free to choose its individuality, where the voice could express its own opinion - *without fear or segregation* - where the word *"no"* was a complete sentence that needed no 'whys' or justification. A time where abuse was not accepted, a time where coercion was rejected, a time where choice and rights were reflected back as a beautiful sight for what it meant to *be* human.

So she sits here in deep despair, with her head in her hands unable to understand *why* humanity has betrayed every birth given freedom that was rightfully theirs? *Why* would any human want to force another into choices that their own heart feels are bad? *Why* can't people see that life is a sacred journey that must be free to be lived with self-truth, self-trust, and self-integrity in *all* experiences had?

I guess she'll never know...
As *her* heart is one of individual flow, that would never force another's life into anything that breaks down their soul.

Lady Balls

She holds a feminine spirit, beautiful in how she moves,
A roar of wild rebellion and sovereign Womanhood,
She's nurturing when is needed, a mother to all lost souls,
With ebbing seasons a-plenty, full of moon tides and daring flows.

Vulnerable in her weakness, showing others they aren't alone,
Authentic in her expression, returning others home,
Deserving of her title with her curves and womanly sway,
Spiritual and sexy in her womanly kinda way.

But don't you be mistaken by her sensuality,
For *she's* a woman of fierceness, when her soul calls her to be,
With lady balls the size of mountains, and courage as high as the sky,
A feminine heart to be feared -

So don't even fucking try!

Breaking Her Chain

No more would she allow herself to go back to patterns of yesterday, whether it be her own or another's. Someone had to disrupt the dysfunctional weave. Someone had to rise up and value who they were - enough to leave. Someone had to be brave, be strong, create right from all the wrong. Someone had to *see*, that life can be lived with authentic beauty, released from the pain, the sadness, the dishonesty.

"My darling...someone had to love themselves enough to break free"

Fierce Heart

Some walk through the storm.
she dances through the fucking fire!

Faded Kaleidoscope

Beautiful had a different meaning.
Inner freedom was felt in ways she had never before known.
Oh how her soul had grown!
Where simplicity was her purpose and peace was now her home.
Dancing into her own forever, away from who she had been and all that once was in-between,
Looking forward with hope, faith, and authentic meaning, as the colours of the past drifted away into the depths of her faded kaleidoscope.
For she had now truly become the woman of *her* dreams,
Gently moving away from the memories of what was before...
And with the deepest of breaths, she just knew -

It wasn't for her, anymore.

Sovereign Revolution

Loving herself, creating her own rules, speaking her truth, and keeping her peace...
These were just some of the beautiful ways her wild heart rebelled everyday against societies brokenness -

Becoming her *own* sovereign revolution of freedom!

Outspoken Woman

If her voice wasn't one of truth they wouldn't try to silence her.

Mother Fucking Wolf Woman

Howling her way through life, like the warrior she is,
Rising from the wounds that *she* herself licked clean,
Thorns beneath her feet, baring battle scars to show –

She's a mother fucking wolf woman from the wild
earth below!

Surrendered Heart

Her heart breaks, cries, retreats, then once again fights courageously for what's right - this is her cycle - as she tries to continue being the voice for the voiceless, the brave for the helpless, the strength for the weak, the eyes for the blind, deeply honouring what it truly means to be human, to live, to break free, to try.

Her heart bleeds for humanity, so she seeks to find the hidden hope that lingers where few dare to look, longing to shine and speak the discovered treasures of truth upon those with dimmed lights. Vulnerable in her pain, desperately giving up herself unto others whilst they throw stones from the rubble which they created, maiming her but not defeated, as she yearns to encourage the awakening in those who still sleep.

Yet her path of purpose leads her to dismay, as many mouths criticise, spit, hate, and shame the mirror of truth she so powerfully shines upon their ignorant eyes, triggering their inner sighs, bursting their 'perfect' bubbles of comfort, conformity, and lies.

But she continues her lonely fight...fighting for all her heart knows to be right, holding faith inside that *'one day soon THEY too will recognise'.*

So she breathes in deep, making nature her temple, whilst her heart breaks and tears fiercely fall into the ground below, retreating once again, as her surrendered heart now clearly sees, societies eagerness to fit in, follow, and 'please', as *she* sits back solemnly, unbind, feeling deep sadness and betrayal from her own kind, wondering why so many seem willing to conform, deny, lay down and die, lacking fight for *our* freedom, empty behind their eyes...

...All the while Mother Earth filling her with understanding inside, for the very first time, why the great Noah welcomed only animals into his Ark to survive.

Deserving

Loving others was what she had always done.
Giving, offering, pouring out her light so that they would not feel the emptiness which she herself has known, yet often forgetting the importance of flowing that same love back into her own feminine heart.
Maybe she didn't feel deserving?
Or maybe she just didn't know how?
Until one day the emptiness became so deep, so broken, so incredibly loud that she could no longer give out to others - *the love, the light, the beauty.*
So instead she returned, she surrendered, she remembered that she *did* deserve it all, and as she saw her open heart clearly for the very first time, she decided to fall more deeply in love…

...In love with herself.

So Howl...

...My Darling...
Scream to the moon if you must.
Sing out all your tears of trauma until each one turns to dust.

Flow Forward

Each movement she made may have been gentle, may have been small, and at times may have felt deeply overwhelming, but this did not matter...
Nor did she care.
For what truly mattered in her heart was the movement, the trying, the kept-promise to herself, and the great courage to 'flow forward' into the beautiful unknown of it all.

The War Paint She Wears

There's no greater war than the one she's already fighting within her own soul. A war with many victories, many heartaches, and many woes.
An inner battle of trust and betrayal to the courage coursing through her feminine veins, forever awakening, returning, and remembering the wild witches that stood before her as she heals the ancestral shame.

For she is a woman who falls like the rest, sometimes doubting the battles she so willingly protests, lost and lonely upon her journey, her search, her everlasting quest.
But weak she is not, even when fallen to her knees, even when broken, when battered, when torn apart from the emotional thieves.

So cut her deep - *if you must* - for you'll soon begin to see, that the war paint she wears upon her face are from the scars *you* made bleed.

The Wisdom She Held Inside...

...Spoke only when she cried,
In solemn tone the truth unknown came falling from her eyes,
When emotions seem to bleed,
When pain was at its most,
When sadness got too much to bear - her truest feelings spoke.

For she has learnt to feel,
Courageously greeting the dark,
Not pushing aside the storms inside seeping from hidden scars,
As it is only truly when,
A woman's heart lets go,
Her wisdom weaves with strength and ease –

Returning her beauty and flow.

She *Does* Care...

...More deeply than you know.
More fiercely than her brokenness allows her to show.
More compassionately than any other broken
human soul.

Yes...

...She *does* care -
She cares for her *own* heart in ways that no-one else
has ever shown.

Sensual Betrayal...

...Penetrating her soul, not allowing her to forget how she has stripped herself bare, as she feels the masculine rage rising within her feminine flow, replacing her softness and surrender with force and fight, unable to retreat to the safety of her womanly womb whilst her familiar primal roar rises up to turn wrong into right.

But she's tired from the strength that won't let her breathe, tired from the inner calling that slowly erodes her craved peace, tired of having to live proud and tall rather than flow like the rivers beauty and ease...

She's so very tired...

In every inch of her essence, every song from her broken sighs, every falling teardrop leaking outwards from her eyes, teardrops that tell the story of her sadness, her struggle, and her unwanted weary climb.

Now all she can do is be still, be free, return to the woman inside of her that she's longing to be, as she vulnerably confronts years of her sensual betrayal, her forgotten truth, her pushed aside inner freedom of innocence and youth, where life made her believe she had no other choice, she had to be the strength, the protection, the loudest voice.

So she drops her heavy sword, healing the battle scars upon her face, as she brings herself back to her beauty, her trust, her womanly grace, creating a sacred space for the divine feminine inside of her to now fully flow, whilst an inner mantra rises up from the soil of Mother Earths nurturing love below, whispering softly to her strength that she *is* safe –

safe to let go.

Not Getting It Right...

...Was beautiful.
Was growth for her soul.
Was the incomplete song that kept her on her toes.
Was the rush, the fall, the awakening behind her eyes,
For 'not getting it right' became the fire for her rise.

Sometimes…

She wants to forget it all, to stop, to pull away from everyone, to birth a totally new path - a path that is simpler, quieter, with deeper healing and returning.

Sometimes she wants to run away, live where nobody can find her, journey into a lost space of forever where only her heartbeat can be heard and the elements are her saviour.

Sometimes she wants to start again, to be unchained from all material things, to offer only herself, her heart, and her essence to the world, to undo years of what's been done, to wake up in a new life, a new morning, a new day.

Sometimes she wants to break free, to let it all go, to fully surrender to the Earth mother, giving herself unto *her - quietly, peacefully, completely* - being of service to *her* will, moving so far away from the ego that there's nothing left but the light.

Sometimes she wants to be forgotten, to be hidden, to be held in the spaces in between the rush, to be loved, to be seen for her soul, and to be so deeply understood and protected by the divine and never let go…

Sometimes.

She Was Beautifully Real...

...Beautiful in how she moved, how she spoke, and how she broke through the chains of adversity. Many admired her – *from afar* - speaking of her authentic beauty as a treasure that's hard to find, envying her courage to be kind – *kind to herself* - dancing to her own created life, unafraid to be different than society's tribe.

She was beautifully real...
...A breath of truth amongst the blanket of lies, awakening those with *un*-awakened eyes, daring to roar where others kept quiet and shy, a beacon of true human-ness – *instinctual, poetic, and wise.*

She was beautifully real...
...falling and rising to her own inner tides and seasons, daring to question and choose *her* hearts way, without justifying her rights and reasons, opening doorways for others to walk through and *see* what's true, a rebel, a fighter, a wild woman, a survivor.

Yes. She was beautifully real –
That was until *she* became beautifully real with *them*.

Away She Flew

The moment she finally let go of every broken memory that kept her spirit caged, was the moment her heart found the wings that carried her away from the weighted tears of yesterday.

She Has The Courage To Be Disliked...

...The strength to be ignored,
The confidence to be criticised, shamed, betrayed and un-adored.

She has the heart to be authentic,
The soul to still be free,
Even when the crowd is trying hard to strip her wild identity.

She has the wisdom to not respond,
The experience to turn her back,
The truth to rise from ignorant eyes - truth that others seem to lack.

She has the voice to stand her ground,
In a world that will never *see,*
How important it is for our souls to express our individuality.

She has the fire to burn the hate,
That flows towards her dance,
Weaving "victory" through the scars *they* bleed with her powerful feminine stance.

Because *she* has the courage to be disliked,
From those that don't understand her fight,
But she will always stay free amongst adversity, till the Earth kisses her heart goodnight.

Awake

Her rebellious awakened heart may be forced to live in a world full of blind slaves, but that doesn't mean she has to become one.

Hold Your Womb...

...Feel *her* strength, allow the beauty of *she* to be reborn into the now. Return, reclaim, and remember *all* that you are - a warrior of the wild, a force of nature, a daughter of Mother Earth - brave in voice, healthy in body, hopeful in heart.

Hold your womb...

...Awaken *her* fight, allow the courage of *she* to be reborn into the now. Return, reclaim, and remember *all* that you are - a liberated soul, uncaged from the crowd, soaring through eternity - rooted in self-trust, peaceful in individuality, beautiful in her own authenticity.

Hold your womb...

...Birth *her* presence, allow the power of *she* to be reborn into the now. Return, reclaim, and remember *all* that you are - a mirror of truth, an essence of light, a unique creation of the divine - bold in presence, primal in actions, intuitive in her flow.

Hold your womb...

My darling,

So you may return, reclaim, and remember to whom you belong.

The Forest Was The Keeper Of Her Smile...

...Returning her to comfort, to truth, to wildness and childlike youth, where magic was possible, life became free, a quiet sacred space for her breath to slow down and *be*.

The roots were the remembrance of her strength...
...grounding her in the inner beauty of the uniqueness of her soul, the courage of her voice, and the right to stand bravely in her individual expression of choice.

The leaves were the movement of her rise...
...bringing the healing to the surface and the love to her pain, so she could hold herself with gentleness and peace once again.

It Doesn't Make Her Weak...

...When she breaks down, howling at the moon, flowing tears that yearn for release, scars broken open, revealing every wound.

It doesn't make her weak...

...When she can't carry on in a moment, when her soul feels tired from the outside world, when her deep trauma arises, reminding her of all the pain from her taken childhood – *the innocent little girl.*

It doesn't make her weak...

...When she walks away or says *no* to anyone or anything that doesn't raise her up, see her value, betrays her trust, or makes her feel unseen, unimportant, and *'just not enough'*.

It doesn't make her weak...

...When she falls, gives up, or forgets her strength, when she can no longer carry on, when each day takes away the ease of her breath, and when her light seems momentarily hidden by the depth of her darkness.

No…

…It doesn't make her weak…

…It makes her brave.

Brave by giving space to her sadness, brave by finding her own way, brave by admitting she is hurting - *unashamed* - brave as she welcomes each rising pain.

Beautifully brave…

…Because she knows that it is only once the shadows in her heart have been truly held, that the beauty of her healing can begin, once again.

Authentic Truth

A woman who has the bravery to be vulnerable with herself is also vulnerable with others.
For it is only *she* who is courageous in heart, is authentic in presence.

Searching...

...Forever searching for the right moment, the right path, the right healing. Craving the fight, the fire, and the burn. With forgotten faith she continues to mourn her inner yearn for all that she is not.

Why can't she see the beauty and bravery she already owns? Why does she still break from the trust inside of her intuitive heart, journeying to find a far away home? Why is she afraid to welcome the peace to stay, to breathe, to flow?

Self-capturing every fall, comfortable in her built up walls, yet longing to birth her million expressions out from the fear that forever rises up, trying to ease her back to familiar earth, until her cycle of broken promises and dreams to herself is once again acknowledged in cowardly defeat, as her old unwanted voice creates false illusions – *proving her to be weak* - making her believe her own inner lies of betrayal.

Yet, deep down, in the womb of her wildness, there was a voice, a voice she so stubbornly ignored in hope it would die, so *she* would not have to *try* and taste the uncomfortable vulnerability of victory, a voice that reminded her she did not need to go searching – *searching for her courage* - for it was already woven within the memories of her soul.

Write, My Darling...

...Write for all the words you cannot speak, for the pain you cannot weep, for the feelings inside your wild soul that you can no longer keep.

Write to understand - *yourself* - to return to your inner story, to stand in your unashamed glory, to rejoice in all that your heart believes to be true, authentic, and holy.

Write for every woman's imperfection, share the beauty of *her* self-acceptance, be the voice for the voiceless so they may stand strong in their own uncaged rebellion.

Write in poetry and prose, write every high and every low, write from your womb, your wild, your own authentic sensual feminine flow.

Write of your forgotten paths, unhealed scars, unloved tears and broken hearts, write of each anger and every laugh, write of regrets that you'll never again start.

Write of intimate desires, of fantasy's and erotic screams, write of your softness and your sighs, your most intimate sacred dreams.

Be courageous with your ink, fuck what others may or may not think, never hold back the *wolf* within *you* to fit in with a world full of sheep.

So write of every victory, write of every rise, write of every envy hiding behind your eyes,
Write of every broken promise, and every broken fall...
Just write,
My darling wild one,
Be brave,
Write it *all!*

Humble Gratitude

Only when the autumn leaves would fall did she
appreciate the blossom -
The same was with her freedom.

Hope...

...She needed it more than ever as she craved the rising light, like a baby does its mother. Longing to feel the weightlessness of life's beauty and breeze. Visualising the world around her flowing freely with faith, unmasked smiles, laughter, hugs, and perfect ease. Praying for shelter, food, money, and human rights for those forgotten so inhumanly, as she prayed for *victory* upon the Earth, whilst asking for chains to be placed around those with darkness, lies, and greed.

Hope...

...Gave her the courage to awaken *'just one more day'*, to not give up, nor give in – *come what may*. Silently screaming for all she couldn't make right, yet never stopping her weary fight. Bringing truth and strength into her restless nights, so morning would birth a new chapter – *full of beauty, freedom, and light.*

Hope...

...Returned her to the Mother divine, the creation of all space and time, reminding her that good *shall* prevail (it always does), and truth *will* once again shine upon the shadows that have took hold of the blind. As it was the Mother that always gifted her through her tears, a whisper growing inside –

"Good always wins, my darling one, so be patient, wild child".

For through the unjust cage, the oppression, the lies, and the soul destroying 'new norm', *hope* was the only fight she had left –
to weather the pain of the storm.

She Wasn't Born To Please...

...To conform, to be a 'team player', to follow the crowd, to live life 'their way', to obey, to lay down like a good girl and follow the rules, to stay oppressed and caged, to make others feel comfortable and safe, to be the same as the rest, to live in fear, to never take risks, to not question, to not speak up.

No.

She wasn't born to please...

...She was born to *dance* the wildness into the hearts of those who sleep.

She Had No Idea…

…About anything or anyone.
Including where she was going.
Her feminine heart of a million seasons had finally surrendered to all the unknowns.
Allowing the pain to ebb, and the peace to flow.
Understanding the world was no longer something she felt a need for, want for, or desire for.
After all -
She still had trouble understanding *herself.*

A Lioness Amongst The Sheep...

...Walking wherever she chose, with pride in each step and freedom in her roar, unafraid to journey into the depths of the unknown, using her feminine instinct to keep her grounded, to keep her strong – *powerful in her presence* - so she may always be guided back home.

Where others cautiously tread with uncertainty, fear, and weakness from ignorant lies, *she* prowls with peace, purpose, and great passion within her truthful spirit, softly soaring – *like an eagle in flight* - through the Earths concrete jungle, whilst holding a quiet confidence, hidden inside.

Visible scars pave her beautiful body from past battles won, scars that show *she* is a survivor, an unbeaten creature, a wild untamed warrior of fight, and a reminder of how far she has courageously come. No woman nor man can strip her bare, break her down, or stop her in her rise, and no attack, no matter how great, can fully open the wounds laying dormant behind her victorious eyes.

For *she* is a lioness amongst the sheep, a woman of the wild, a rebel with scars of remembrance to what others are too scared to allow, reminding those who may draw near through her prowess of deep freedom from pain -

"Hear me ROAR and hear me RISE - again, and again, and again"

With A Book In Her Hand...

...She lay amongst the wildflowers, soaking up the warming sunshine upon her back, taking herself away from the place she was in. With every word read and every page turned, her soul re-wrote its own story, a story where she was free, where she was unbroken, where she was liberated from the cage and the pain of the world. A story where she could be anyone, say anything, express however she chose. There were no rules, no leaders, and no teachers to pave the way. There was only *her* way, *her* truth, and *her* path, filled with colour, craziness, and the beautiful unknown of it all.

With a book in her hand...

...She became someone else, someone new, someone unseen, yet so deeply real and true. A woman whose heart was wide open to every risk, flowing through her existence, making her feel truly alive. Through the stories hidden within each page, she found another version of herself, returning her to an inner home, far, far away from the now. A home where she could slow down and catch her breath, a home where she understood the true meaning of happiness, and a home where each moment became the healing of her brokenness.

With a book in her hand...

...She could forget it all – *the hypocrisy, the lies, the ignorance and the denial* - from an abiding society with blind eyes, oppressed minds, and masked smiles. The more she read, the more her own integrity and intuition was fed, taking her further away from the inauthentic-ness of the cowardly crowd, back to her wanderlust wild spirit, her uncaged soul, her free thinking mind, and her courageous rebellious voice, spoken loud and proud...
As it was only with a book in her hand, laying amongst the wildflowers, that her heart could finally return and surrender to the true story of *her*.

Naked Heart

There is nothing more beautiful within this world than a woman who is courageous enough to wear all her broken pieces upon her skin.

She Had To Fall Back Into Her Faith...

...To raise her high when her heart was buried and broken.
To bring back her smile...if only for a while when her eyes would weep.
To be the oxygen that kept her breathing in the aliveness of life, even when her soul wanted to give up in defeat.
To be the courage of a whisper deep inside, the voiceless voice that could no longer be denied, and the gentle embrace that held her tightly when she cried.
To be the roar of the fire fuelling her to get up when she was on her knees.
To be the cooling waters that calmed her hateful anger towards those that tried to keep her weak.
To be the gentleness of the breeze, softening her skin – *without and within* - when her walls were built up thick from protection, pain, and misfortune.
To be the miracle, the hope, the *one* truth that always spoke, the very thing that kept her rising authentically through the mirrors and smoke.

For this was her only choice, her only voice, and her only truth that helped tenderly place all her broken pieces back together, as it was only by falling deeply *back* into her faith, that she knew she would slowly fall back into her freedom too.

Loving Her Back To Life

She wasn't created for this world, although it sometimes felt like this world was created for her - *her* eyes, *her* healing, *her* pain and beauty within every unspoken feeling. A temple to remind her of where she belongs, a far-away feeling bringing her closer to home, a hidden memory of another life flowing through the breeze, the scent, the rain the sun and the rooted trees, all whispering into her tired soul - "*come walk with me, my darling one, let me show you where to go*".

She didn't need to understand, she didn't need to struggle or cry, she didn't need to fight, to question, or to try, all she needed were the whispers that Mother Earth poured into her restless feminine womb, whispers that broke the lies and bought her back to truth.

As it was only in natures embrace that she felt her true self return. With sacred ground beneath her feet and the great mother holding every broken heartbeat, she felt free – *free to be open, to be vulnerable, to be soft, to be enough, to fall back into a weightlessness of unconditional love…*

Loving her back to life.

Spiritually Human

She was a sacred, sovereign, spiritual soul,
With wildness in her heart and freedom in her flow,
An expression of liberation, awakening, and truth,
A woman of deep integrity –

{and a little 'fuck you!'}

January Rain...

...Gently falls down as she gazes towards the winter sky, hope and pain captured behind her big brown gypsy eyes, allowing the waters from above to carry her soul away from all the injustice, darkness, and lies – *to a place of wild freedom, beauty, and love* - where the peace in her soul cannot be denied. Arms outstretched like a fallen child, crying for her mother to hold her in a loving embrace, praying through every drop that falls gently across her naked face, to bring down wrath and winds of change, to give the gift of courage where cowards remain, and to awaken the hearts who still ignorantly sleep upon this earthbound plane.

Broken, bruised, betrayed and used, but still fearless in her fight, as her own inner unbound universe roars inside, not allowing her to forget *who* she is born from and all *she* knows to be right, forever held by the moon, the sun, the Earth, and the eternity of the night.

So she runs through her stormy fields alone, barefoot and free, running away from all she calls home, running away from a life she no longer wants to know, running to find a place her heart can wildly roam.

Not stopping to look back,
Nor slowing to feel her pain,
As she continues to search for the beauty of light,
hidden within her January rain.

Don't Give Her A Gun…

…Instead place a pen in her hand, for her words can do more damage than a gun ever can.

How Much Is Enough?...

...Before her wild heart breaks in two,
Before the freedom within her soul comes
screaming through,
Before she stands up and fights for all which is
rightfully hers,
Rather than sit back caged and oppressed - blindly
following the herd.

How much is enough?...

...Before she *sees* the lies and the mass control,
Before she listens to her *own* intuition telling her
where to go,
Before she understands that life *is* one big risk,
A risk that she's meant to dive into, explore, and
unapologetically live.

How much is enough?...

...Before she makes her *own* rules, guidance,
and choice,
Before she rips that pointless mask off her face,
honouring the uniqueness of *her* birth given voice,
Before she realises that this world is led by those

with greed in their eyes,
Behind 'man made' fears, injustice, hypocrisy,
and intentional lies.

So tell me, my darling -

How much *is* enough before you rise up and *live,*
or lay down and *die?*

New Paths, Forgotten Memories...

...This was her future. Her re-birthing. Her only way to flow forward into a life of beauty, truth, and healing, a life that had always been awaiting for her to let it all go - the sadness, the hurt, the unjust actions and voices, the wrongful choices, and the many shadows from others of her past, all masking her own light from creating its truest form.

New paths, forgotten memories...

...A way for her to be free, to be herself, to be all that she longed to be. By sailing down new rivers and forgetting all traces of storms left behind, storms that were created by others, storms that were placed upon *her* peace, and storms that were never hers to weather. Allowing nothing but truth, love, respect, and authentic hearts to sail alongside her.

New paths, forgotten memories...

...The only choice that would now make her smile, give her back her power, awaken her wildness, and raise her beautiful spirit into its wholeness, was by forgetting to remember it all...

Every, little, thing.

So she did...

...She cried a river for every hurtful word, she broke into pieces for every unwelcomed energy, she stopped caring about those who only saw her as they chose, and she ripped out the thorns from every unkind friend, family, and foe, as she walked gently upon the Earth, awakened through the wild flowers, allowing the sunbeams to warm her smile with every step, sweetly surrendering to all she could never control.

It was only then, in this moment of surrender, her tired soul took the deepest of breaths, whilst the Earth Mother held her tightly, gifting her strength to walk into new light, new chapters, and new blossoming beginnings.

So with courage in her heart and peace behind her eyes, she proudly burnt away the chains. With every scar healed the more the Earth revealed, that is was only by embracing these new paths and forgotten memories, that her heart would finally be free from the pain.

When She Felt Heard...

...Her soul was more able to express itself, her songs voice spoke with deeper calmness, and her unsettled heart became more courageously rooted in her own feminine truth.
As her vulnerability *received* acceptance, compassion, understanding, and nurturing love, she began to feel held, to feel healed, to feel hopeful, allowing *her* to give this same flow of freedom back out to where it was birthed.

When she felt heard...

...Her peace pushed through the pain, her strength arose through the struggle, her tears transformed into an untold treasure, and her trauma began to deeply disappear.

As her brokenness was given space to be gently placed back together, her beauty began to blossom, to flourish, to become whole, bringing each one of her seasons into completion - *a cycle of remembrance, recognition, and return.*

When she felt heard...She let go of the fight.

Gratitude Drew Her In…

...Like a moth to the flame.
Those with open hearts, kind mouths, mountains of appreciation and authentic beauty deeply scented within their essence, made her want to *give* more, to *share* more, to *love* more, and to *help* more when help was needed.
She adored the souls who *gave* as well as *took*, she praised those who were *brave* enough to be *this* beautiful, and she made time for those who were wise enough to see the sacredness of *her* generosity.

But she was no fool…

…Quietly laying behind her giving heart, behind her truth, behind her forever flowing gifts, she could *see* who deserved it and who didn't, she could *feel* who's energy was authentic and true, she could *hear* by the words which another spoke whether they were someone of respect, honour, and gratitude.

And it was only in these awakening moments, the moments that her giving nature was casually being pushed aside, disrespected, ignored, and forgotten by those with lying intentions, selfish sighs, expectations and un-appreciation hiding behind their greedy eyes, that Mother Earth called upon her wild instinct to rise, reminding *her* voice to howl, to roar, to unapologetically fight, as her sacred energy and intuitive soul shivered underneath the smoothness of her calm skin, making her retract and retreat within *-like a wild bucking horse -* whispering through her inner knowing*"never gift to this person again"*.

For it was always and only the hearts of *true* gratitude, that drew her *own* heart in the most.

Her Song Of Freedom

She knew that her wild spirit was only placed upon this beautiful Earth for such a short time, as she danced through her individual path, fighting through the lies, acknowledging that she will never truly know if today was her last, she will never truly *see* the 'what's when's and how's', and she will never truly *be* in control of the many unseen risks, surrounding the now.

But regardless of this external cage, endlessly playing with her own inner perfect storm, the 'who's right' and 'who's wrong', the division, the 'new norm', the rules, the man-made unjust laws, and the many different voices scorned...
She would forever dance her own dance, instead of the beat of another's,
She would forever scream "victory!" for her future sisters, daughters, and mothers,
She would forever stand for her own individual choice, instead of waiting to be dictated to, scripted to, or 'saved',
She would forever stand for integrity and honour, instead of hiding blindly behind the many masks made,
She would forever stand for listening to her incredible

birth given intuition, instead of the ever-changing noise of the crowd,
She would forever stand for truth, justice, and liberty, instead of conformity, oppression, and a life that's been wrongly stripped down...
Forever holding freedom instead of fear,
Smiles instead of tears,
Unapologetically standing in her own woman-made frontier,
Willingly opening herself for judgment,
Breaking the rules, the laws, and creating her own,
Releasing those who no longer shared her dance, even if this meant sometimes standing alone,
Because this was *her* one precious life, a life that she knew would one day be gone.

So, when her moment finally came to make that spiritual journey back to her everlasting home, *she* would reminisce on the past with peace, with pride, with no regrets lingering behind her rebellious eyes, as her earthly breath allows her heart to sweetly sing out her song of freedom, one last time –

"Through all the wrongs,
Through all the fights,
I NEVER *gave up my rights!"*

"I Don't Belong Here"

Her tired awakened eyes gazed solemnly upon the vast starlit sky, whilst moonbeams trickled gently down, caressing her voluptuous womanly thighs, taking in endless stories of every curve, every dip, and every rise, as she lay there broken - *free, naked, and wild* - innocent like a new born child.

Sinking into the Earth, desperate for connection in her vulnerable surrendering of self, pleading with the softness of the mothers soil to let her back in to all which she once was, unbinding her from the skin she now wears, longing for it to be stripped back bare and begin her journey again...

A journey into forever,
A release into an endless flow of freedom,
And an open doorway into a spiritual sacredness of eternity.

So her brown eyes wept, for all that she longed for and all that was no more, allowing every tear to soak into the fertile ground below in hope it would be heard, healed, and resealed, then buried and burnt from the fires of her screams, screams that broke out from the deepest part of her wounded womb with a sorrowful song of pain that howled out from within her weakened beating heart -

"Take me...
Take me away from it all.
I don't belong here.
And I never did"

When The Tide Had Turned...

...Her tears became her smile, her fight became her freedom, her pain became her peace, and her past became the building blocks of every battle won.

Through the seasons, the struggle, the drowning emotions, the lost breath, and the heaviness of the ocean weighing down upon her sinking soul, somewhere deep inside of her, within the eye of the storm, she caught glimmers of calming waters, embraced with moments of stillness and surrender, all returning her to truth.

When the tide had turned...
...She was filled with the beauty of her future, heart-felt hope, and a million visions of her *'why'*, all rushing through her creative essence, pouring life back into her empty vessel.

Wounds were healed, scars sweetly sealed, and courage called her to fight, to try, to not give up, to hold her mighty sword high with pride and poise once again, to scream out undefeated, to swim against the crashing salty waters forever forcing her to stay beneath the surface - hidden, ashamed, and quiet...

...But she would not stay sunken in the murky depths,
She would not stay silent in the shallow breaths,
And she would not stay broken in her brokenness...

Only when the tide had turned, she remembered her forgotten shore, she remembered all she was once before, she remembered to forget no-more, as she peacefully lay upon the sunlit golden sand, gazing up at the clear blue skies passing softly above her beaten but victorious eyes, she heard the sea whispering through each lapping wave –

"Breathe deeply darling one...
For you are home, you are home, you are home"

Only When...

...She wants to live, rather than 'just exist',
Only when she wants to take daring risks, rather than stay 'safe' and caged,
Only when she wants to embrace life's natural fear, rather than trying to control it,
Only when she wants to stand with personal integrity, rather than crowd conformity,
And only when her heart awakens to what it truly means to be free...

...She will *never* want to settle for anything less.

The Earth Belongs To No-one…

…She is her own unique, beautiful creation,
Not designed by 'man',
Nor birthed by woman.
She alone stands free.
Flourishing and blossoming as wildly as *she* chooses,
Nothing and no-one to answer to,
As her body evolves and dances through her own created nature -
Uncaged,
Untamed,
Unapologetically flowing wherever her soul carries her -

"Oh how I long for that kind of freedom"

Rebel For Life

She never wore their mask, she shoved the needle up their arse, and with a deep rebel breath she gave life the finger, living just as *she* chose to be –

Wild, awake, free!

Lavender Oil And Incense...

...Reminder her what's real,
Burning scents beside her as she surrenders back to heal,
Familiar with this ritual of returning to her heart,
A cycle that sacredly grounds her, aligning what's broken apart.

Lavender oil and Incense...
...From mothers flourishing Earth,
Allowing the old to burn away so her new may be re-birthed,
Sinking deeply down within the truth that she once denied,
Honouring whispers of forgotten fires hidden gently behind her eyes.

Lavender oil and incense...
...Flow forth her freedom of choice,
Awakening her once again to rise up with courage and voice,
A voice she had forgotten,
A truth she had suppressed,
Then lavender oil and incense bring her heart back home to rest.

Even On The Most Beautiful Of Days…

…The sunshine within her soul can still become hidden from the shade.
No matter how hard she smiles,
No matter how much she prays,
For she is only a woman -

Imperfectly made.

She Remembers...

...Away from the posts, the likes, the comments, the messages, the virtual masks, craved attention, falsified truths, and opposing opinions, her heart quietly but courageously broke away from it all, so *she* would remember what it truly means to be human, what it truly means to live in each moment, what it truly means to unfollow the crowds voice, and what it truly means to be back home in the Earth, seeking validation from no-one but herself, with nothing but nature and her own inner truth to muse upon.

She remembers...

...What play and childhood fun feel like whilst she sits contentedly in her own world, her own expression, her own passions, unaffected by the outside, un-pressured to keep up, and unapologetic in her rebellious wildness as she dances throughout each day how *she* chooses, hidden away from curious minds, prying people, and fake connections from those who she doesn't really know.

She remembers...

...The beauty of sitting by a fire, a herbal tea, an incense burning, cosy and comforted in her own unseen moment of healing, ritual, and honour of the Earth mother, with only her wild hair, naked face, bare feet, beating heart, and vulnerable whispers present. No video to share, no beautiful captured image to show off, and no 'forced memory' for her ego to post to the world...

...Just *her.*

And with this beautiful betrayal of the crowds way, the 'digital devil', and the online oppression, she abundantly remembers the gift and sacredness of what it means to be still, to be true, to be her...

...to be *free!*

Her Intuition Was All The Truth She Needed…

…To awaken her, to encourage her, to question every word, every act, and every person that crossed her path, allowing the beauty and liberation of 'self-responsibility' to howl through her instinctual free soul…an innate gift given to every human, yet, this inner truth, this inner power, now so carelessly pushed aside by both women and men, happily abandoning themselves to serve the voice of another, abandoning *their* truth and *their* emotions, just in case it 'offends'.

Where others would follow the 'guidance', the 'rules', the dictatorship from 'those in charge', *she* would follow her own hearts voice, her own judgment, and her own inner whispers, flowing through her courageous beating heart like a sea of emotions, an eternal energy of knowledge created from the day she was born.

Where others would willingly live fearful of what the outside voices would preach, *she* would live surrendered in peace, knowing that *her* truth comes from a space more honest and real than any human mouth could ever speak.

Where others would stick to the books, keep within the picture, and stay within the lines, *she* would wildly colour with every dam crayon in the box, creating her own life's image, expressing authenticity with every ounce of her soul, living fully and freely where others choose to live oppressed in fear.

Why?...

...Because *she* knew, through all of the noise, the 'who's right and who's wrong', and the lies behind the ignorant eyes, that the only way she could truly be free was to always be herself –
Forever using the deep intuition of her wild, womanly heart to guide her.

When It Is All Over...

...She shall sit back,
with a smile in her heart,
knowing that *she* never gave up what was rightfully hers.

"When, My Darling, *When*?"

When did you start unloving yourself and thinking more of others?
When did you begin to believe everyone else's opinions were more important than your own?
When did you get told that speaking, expressing, and living *your* truth, with *your* intentions, *your* humour, and *your* choice of words was bad?
When did you start apologising to everyone and dishonouring yourself?
When did someone else's 'being offended' become a signal for you to bow your head in shame and stop being *you*?
When did you allow the voices of society to drown out your own?
When did you begin waiting for another to set *you* free?
When did you place the responsibility of *your* life in the hands of another?
When did you get told that it's selfish, unkind, or uncaring to think of yourself?
When did you lose your own identity and merge with the crowds?
When did you allow the emotional dirt from another's pain to muddy *your* peace?

When did 'your way' become wrong, and everyone else's 'way' become right?
When did you forget the importance of integrity, independence, and individuality?
When did you stop asking questions, seeking the truth, and discovering your own hearts answers?
When did you forget how to embrace the risks and *live* in this short gift called life?
When did you lose the beauty, uniqueness, and incredible essence of authentic expression that you were born with? The very thing that makes you, *you?*

When, my darling,
When?

The Leaves In Autumn

The change was already here.
The new birthing was oh so clear.
Without her even doing a thing, the Mother *released* her from everything -
Bad souls, wrong paths, heavy people.
Allowing her to *breathe*, to *see*, with peace and authentic clarity, the beauty and inner freedom now emerging within her intuitive courageous heart.
Finally letting go of what once was -

Just
Like
The
Leaves
In
Autumn.

She Was Busy Doing Nothing...

...And everything all at once. Walking amongst nature, taking slower breaths, listening to the bird song, to the silence of the Earth. Feeling who *she* was becoming, surrendering to painful decisions of the '*whys, when's,* and *how's*', patiently allowing her heart to catch up with the *now.*

She was busy doing nothing...
...Being selfish, saying '*no*' to what and who didn't feel good for her soul. Ignoring the phone calls, the messages, and the connections, letting responsibilities go, whilst *she* allowed herself to flow into much needed time for her own beautiful needs, honouring *her* healing - unapologetically so.

She was busy doing nothing...
...Creating her soul, understanding *who* this woman now was in the mirror – *incomplete but still whole.* Expressing her many faces so she could rediscover herself, in every crease, every pain, and every broken piece, like a story untold, softly seeing the truth of her own inner *Queen*-dom, placing her pieces back together with courage, faith, and feminine freedom.

She was busy doing nothing...
...Crying it out, releasing every tear, every pain, and every sadness from lingering fears, from heartbroken years, from shadows and seasons that would sometimes draw near, authentically embracing the love, the life, and the light her heart deserved, the feeling she had longed for, and the newness she had desperately longed to birth, so she could fully embrace the nurturing peace that was also longing for *her.*

She was busy doing nothing...
...And her *nothing,* was ok.

Silence…

…Would sometimes sound so loud to her heart, for she needed the noise to drown out the pain she hadn't quite yet healed.

It's Ok, My Darling...

...Let *her* go...
The woman you once were -
For *who* you are becoming is trying to be born.

I Wonder…

…What if I told her that her life would end tomorrow, that her heartbeat would beat its last song, that every little part would be over, that there would be no more *her*…

…Would she still walk around complying, doing as she is told to 'save lives', wearing a mask across her beautiful face, keeping her distance from the ones she loves, whilst limiting access to those closest to her to 'stick to the numbers', just because some man in a suit told her to?

I wonder…

…Would she still hold back from living, from taking risks, from being a *free* wild woman, *or*, would she fearlessly *live*, take chances, *breathe* it all in, courageously squeezing out every ounce of her precious life that she could?

I wonder…

…Would she happily listen to what she's being told, accepting the dictatorship placed upon *her* life, willingly following those in power, *or* would she listen to her own hearts inner guidance, rebel against the crowd, make her own health choices and decisions, and live in a way that brings *her* wild freedom and peace?

Mostly, I wonder...

...How differently she would act if she was awake to this one human truth - *that no-one knows when today is their last* - instead of continuing to act like *her* life goes on forever *'if only she follows the rules'*...

...I wonder...don't *you?*

Meet Her There...

...Where the silence is speaking,
Where the brokenness is healing,
Where the scars are gently weeping,
Just enough to share.
Where the trauma turns to treasure,
Where the love goes on forever,
Where we stand as one together...

...Where there is peace -
Meet her there.

Someday…

…All the frustration, all the wrong, all the sadness, all the silent screams, all the tears, and all the ever growing fears inside of her beautifully wild heart will be nothing more than a memory of shadows, an inner book of a closed chapter, a pain that has passed, and an old beaten cage that *she* courageously broke free from.

Someday, she will look back and remember –

"I never gave up"

Remember Her...

...When the soul is sinking, when the darkness overtakes, when the smiles and the laughter become too hard to fake.

Remember her...
...The woman who never gave up, the woman who has been before, the woman who authentically arose through every weeping scar with her wild courageous roar.

Remember her...
...For *she* is still within you, my darling –

A great rose amongst the thorns.

About the Author

Gaia Rose

Mother, wife, wild woman...survivor!

Gaia Rose is a deeply expressionate, intuitive, force of nature - *through her written word, her voice, or her art* – forever creating her own rules. A seeker of truth and a fighter for freedom who encourages other women to always create their own path whilst living authentically and courageously from their individual heart.

www.gaiarose.co.uk

CPSIA information can be obtained
at www.ICGtesting.com
Printed in the USA
LVHW022002120422
716028LV00006B/392

9 781838 055462